ABC's BODY PARTS AND ORGANS BOOK
FOR KIDS

INTRODUCTION

The human body is considered one of the greatest things on the universe, as it works like a machine and it is consists of several organs and parts of different size, shape and function, but all of these organs have one and only goal that is to keep you alive. In this book you will learn about some of the most important parts and organs in the human body and its functions and placement with beautiful illustarations, and most importantly, you will learn the english alphabet while learning about the human body.

A is for...

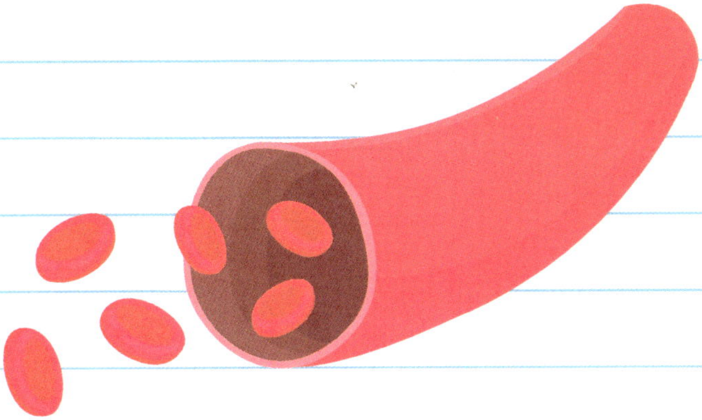

ARTREY

An artery is a blood vessel, that transports blood from the heart to all parts and organs of the body.

B is for... BLOOD

Blood is a red liquid that circulates in all arteries of the body, it is made up of red blood celles, white blood cells, plasma and platelets.

C is for...

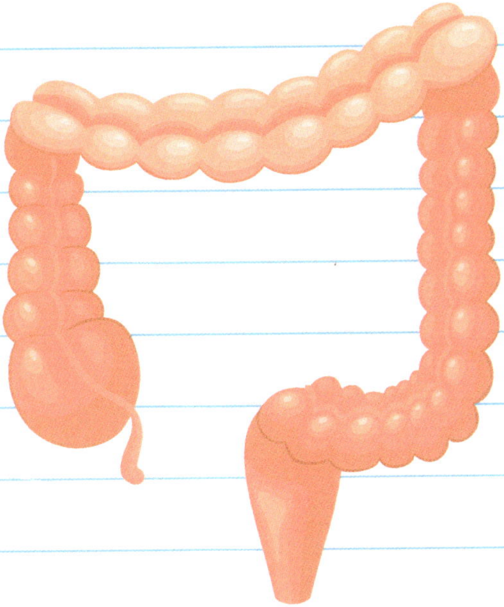

COLON

Colon is a part of the intestines and exactly it's the longest part of the large intestine, and it is located at the end of the gastrointestinal tract.

D is for...

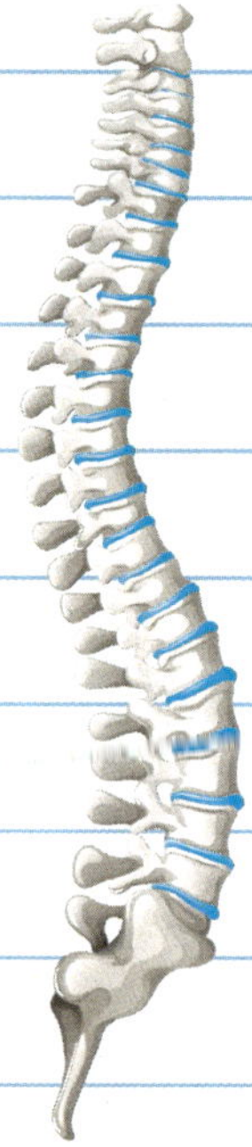

DORSAL SPINE

Dorsal spine is a serie of vertebras that located in your back, it is considered as the most important part of the skeleton.

E is for...

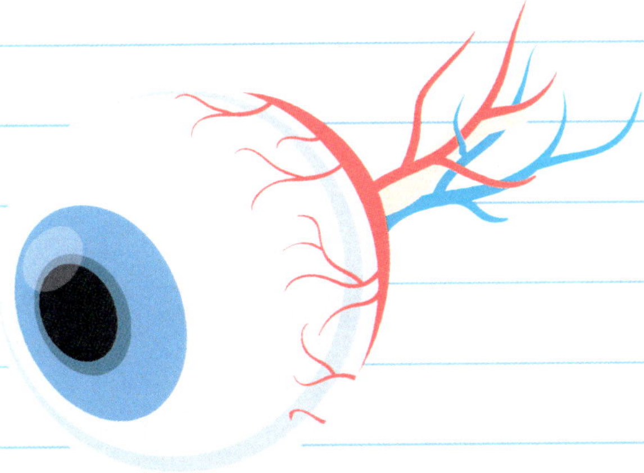

EYE

The eye is the only organ that gives you the sence of sight, it is consisting of several parts including the iris.

F is for...

FINGERPRINT

Fingerprints are those little lines on your fingers, each person has a unique fingerprint, and it is used to identify peoples.

G is for...

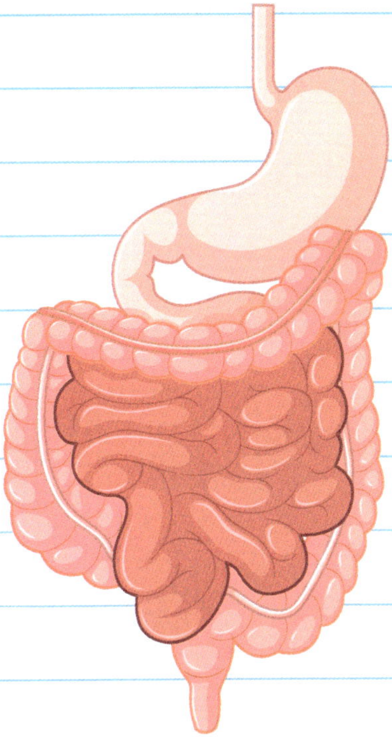

GASTROINTESTINAL TRACT

Gastrointestinal tract is the organ responsible for digesting food and absorbing energy and nutrition from it, it is a group of organs including the stomach and the intestines.

H is for...

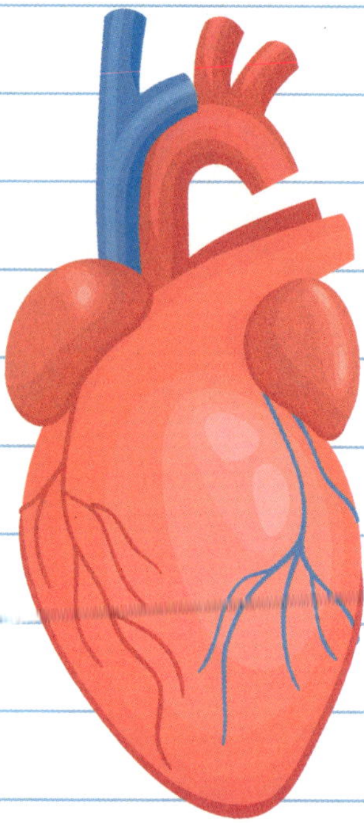

HEART

The heart is the hollow muscular organ that is responsible for pumping the blood through the arteries to all body parts and organs in a systematic way.

I is for...

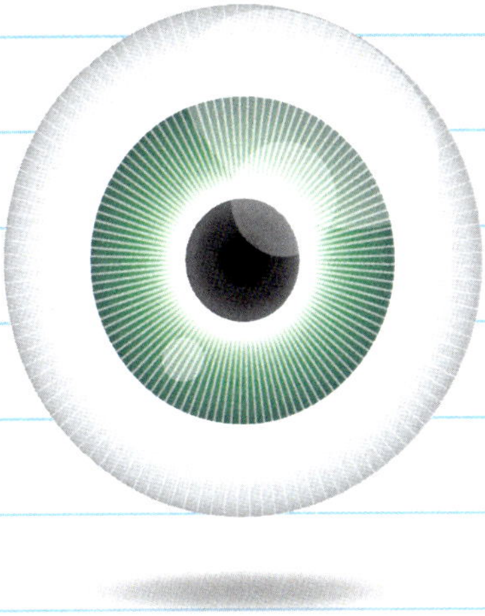

IRIS

The iris is the colored part of the eye, and it responsible for determining the diameter and the size of the pupil and also controlling the amount of light that is reaching the retina.

J is for...

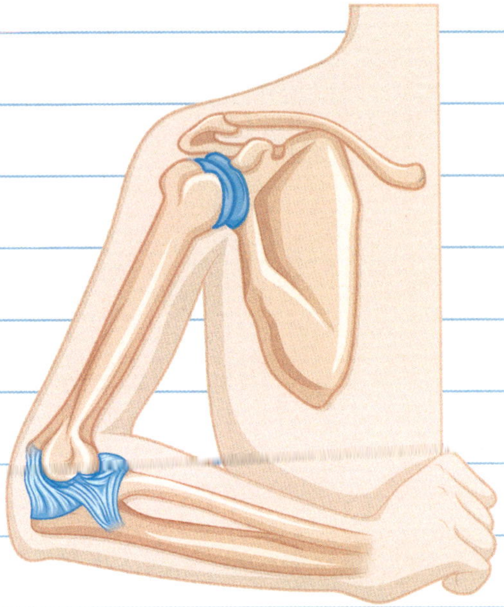

JOINT

Joints are a group of parts that separate two or more bones, it is essential for building the skeleton.

K is for...

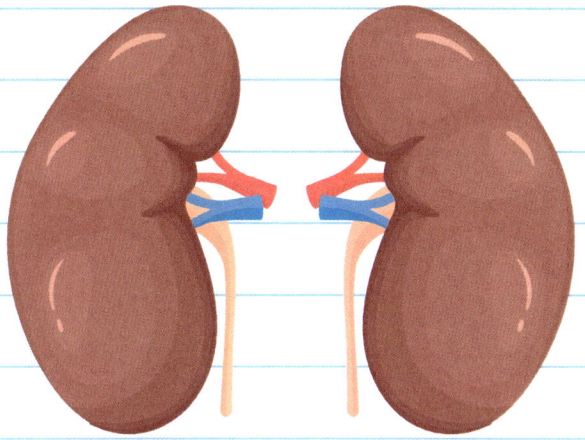

KIDNEYS

The kidneys is the organ that is responsible for removing waste products from the blood and also for produce urine, and it is located in the right and left side of the abdomen.

L is for...

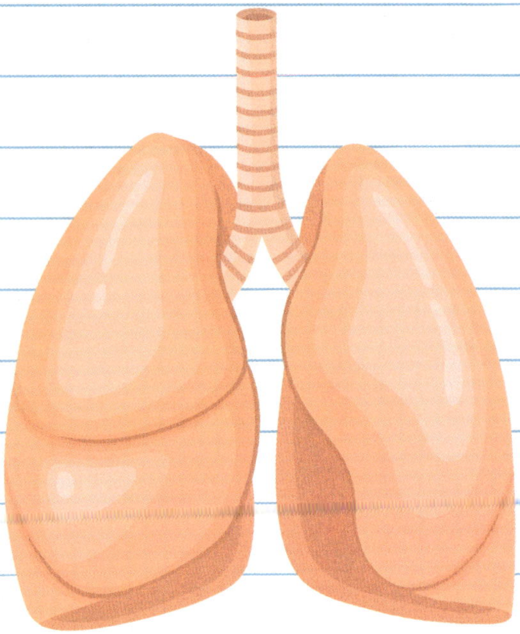

LUNGS

The lungs are the most important part of the respiratory and breathing system, as they are responsible for removing the carbon dioxide from the body and pumping oxygen to the blood, the lungs are found inside the chest.

M is for...

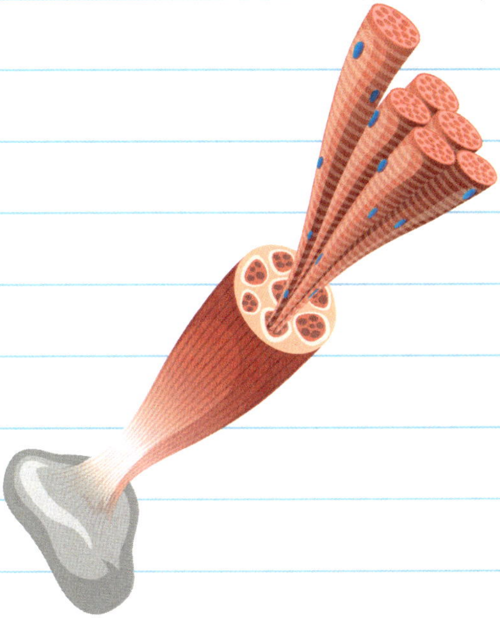

MUSCLE

Muscle is a group of fibres that connects two bones and which you use when you make a movement, it is considered as a skeleton engine.

N is for...

NOSE

The nose is also a part of the respiratory system, which is responsible for getting air in and out of the lungs, and it is also responsible for the sence of smell.

O is for...

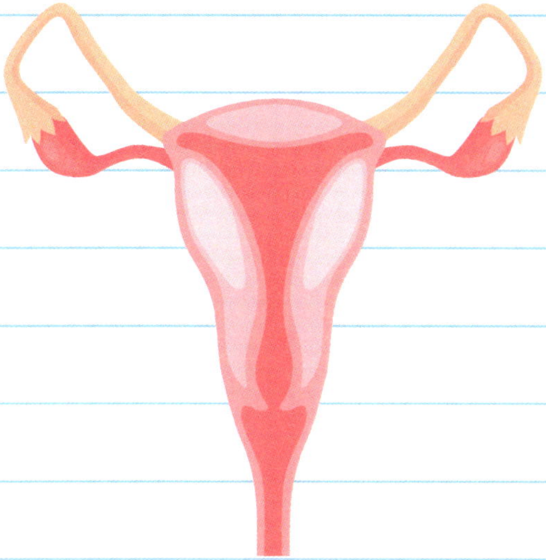

OVARY

The ovary is the one of the most important parts of the female reproductive system, it is responsible for the production of ova and the production of female hormones such as estrogen.

P is for...

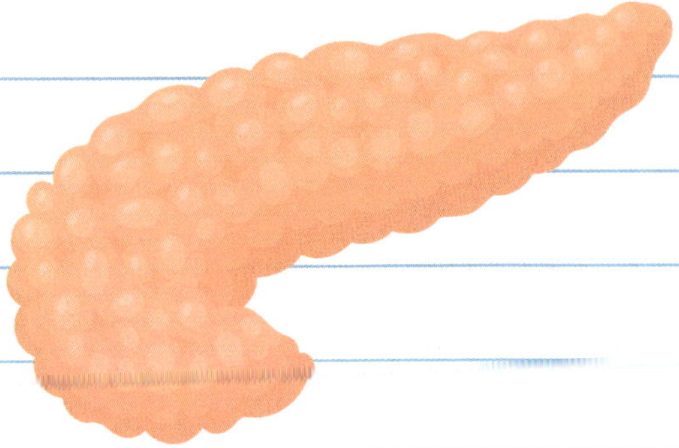

PANCREAS

The pancreas is a large gland located behind the stomach close to the first part of the small intestine, and it helps the stomach to digest food by secreting the digestive juices to the small intestine.

"Q is for..."

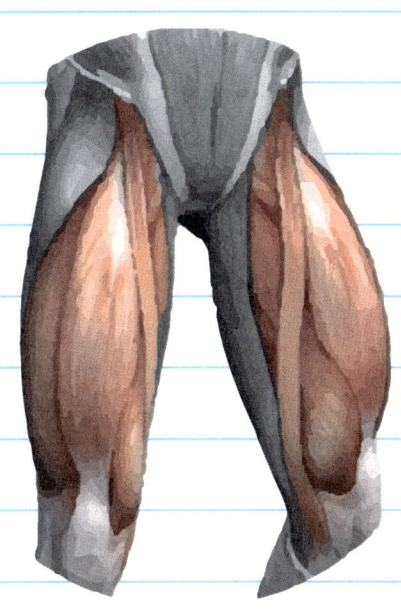

QUADRICEPS

Quadriceps is a large muscle consisting of four muscles combined together and located in the front of your thigh.

R is for...

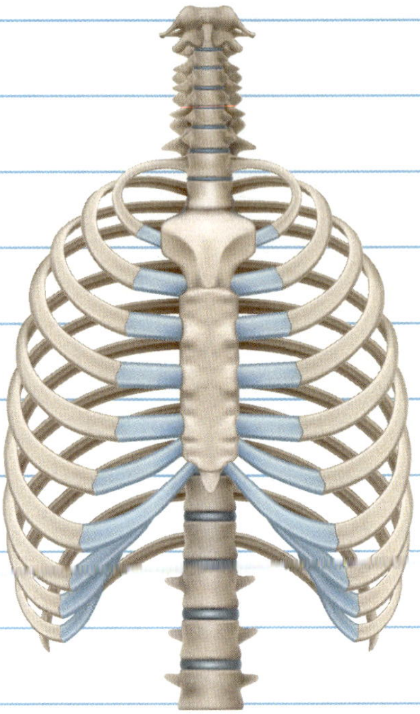

RIB CAGE

The rib cage is a group of bones and ribs connected to the dorsal spine and forms a wall to protect internal organs such as the heart and lungs.

S is for...

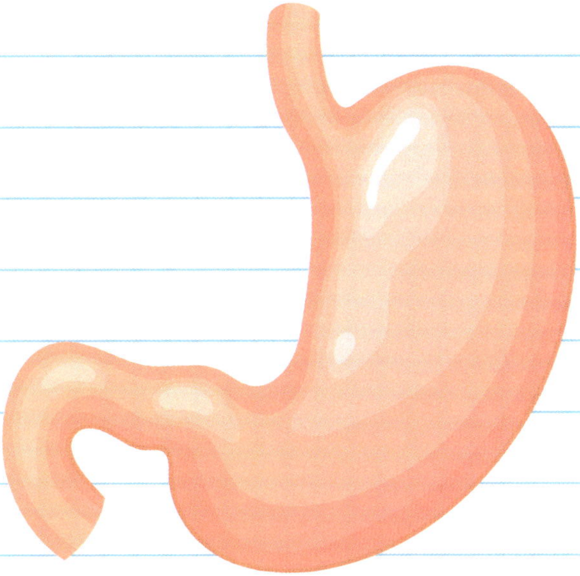

STOMACH

The stomach is the main organ of the digestive system, which digests and passes food through the intestines to absorb energy and nutrients from it.

T is for...

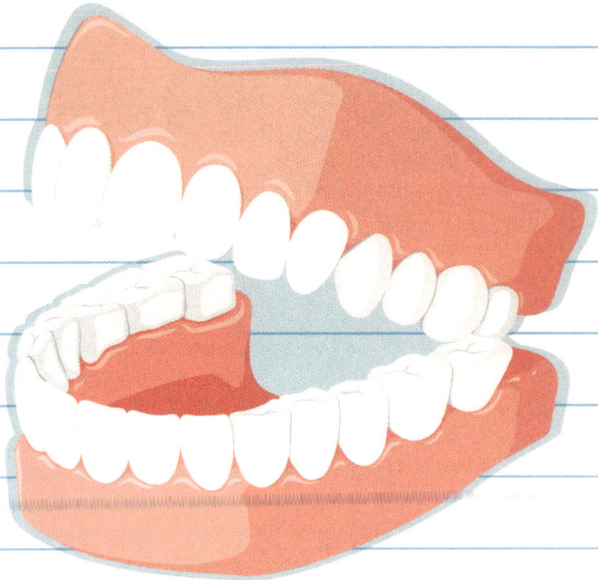

TOOTH

The teeths are made of hard bones, and they are formed in the form of a wall from the top to the bottom, to cut and chew food.

U is for...

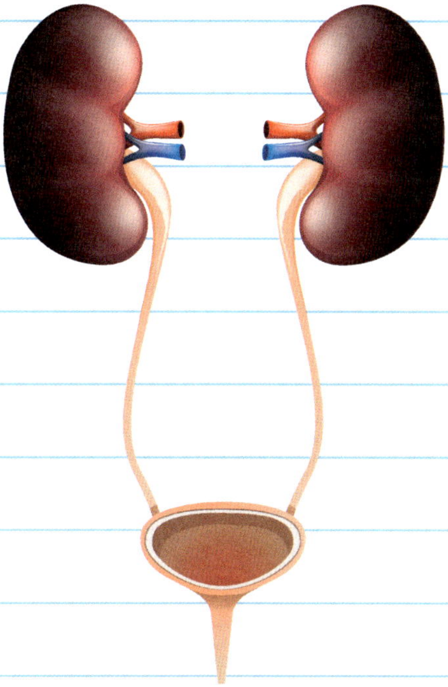

URINARY TRACT

the urinary tract consists of a group of organs and parts starting with two kidneys to the bladder, through which the urine passes.

V is for...

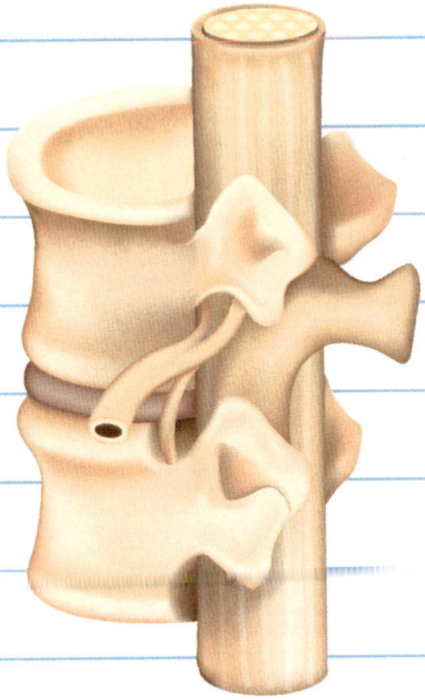

VERTEBRA

The Vertebra are small bones with a complex structure, that make up your Drosal spine, and it is also located in your back.

W is for...

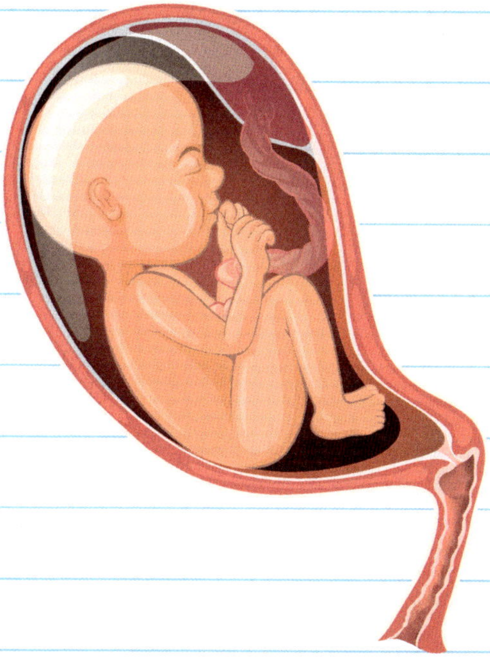

WOMB

The Womb is the organ that a baby grows in during the pregnancy (when a woman is pregnant).

X is for... XIPHOID PROCESS

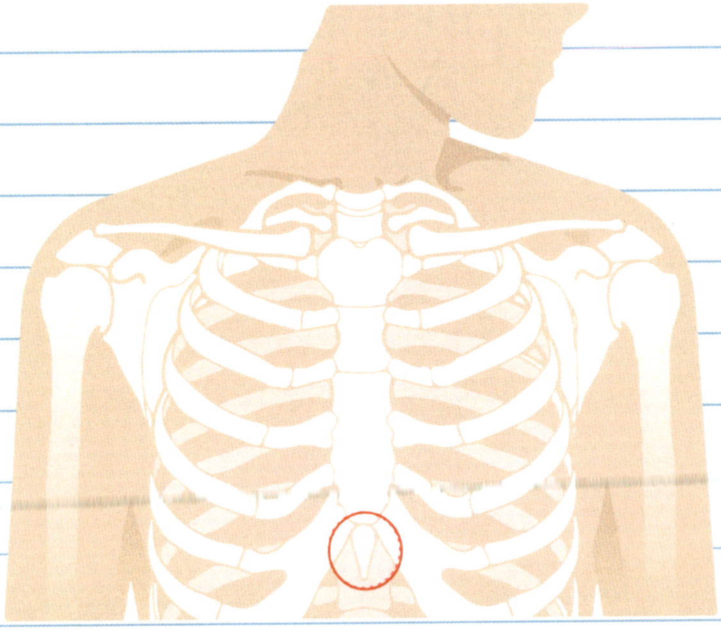

The xiphoid process is considered the smallest bone in the rib cage, as it is a cartilage that develops at the age of adulthood to become a bone, and is found in the cross ribs from inside the rib cage.

Y is for...

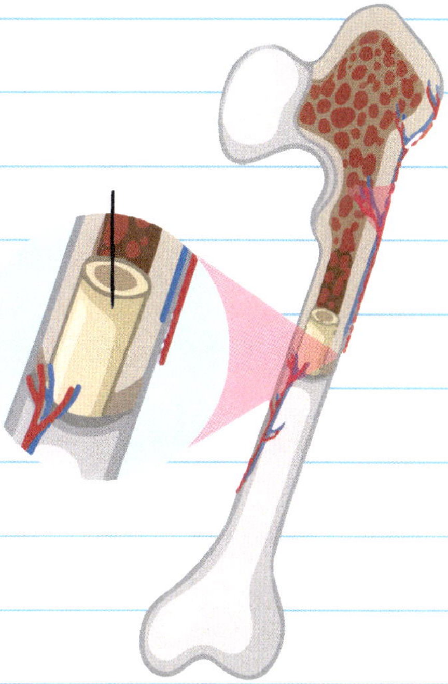

YELLOW MARROW

A Yellow marrow is located inside the long and large bones in adults, and it is made up of fat.

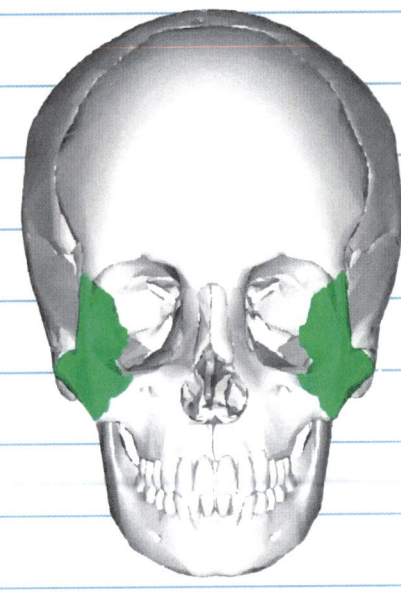

ZYGOMATIC

The zygomatic bone is located on both of the right and the left side of the face, and it forms the bones of the cheeks.

FUN FACTS ABOUT HUMAN BODY

1- The human body contains more than 100 trillion cells in adults.

2- The human nose can remember more than 50,000 smell.

3- The average of breaths that an adult takes a day is over than 20,000.

4- The average of blood liters that the Kidneys process a day is 200 liters.

5- The human adults body can excrete about 1.42 liters of urine each day.

6- The human dorsal Spine contain 33 vertebra.

7- The human adult's body weight is made up of 50 percent of water.

8- The human brain contain about 100 billion neurons in adults.

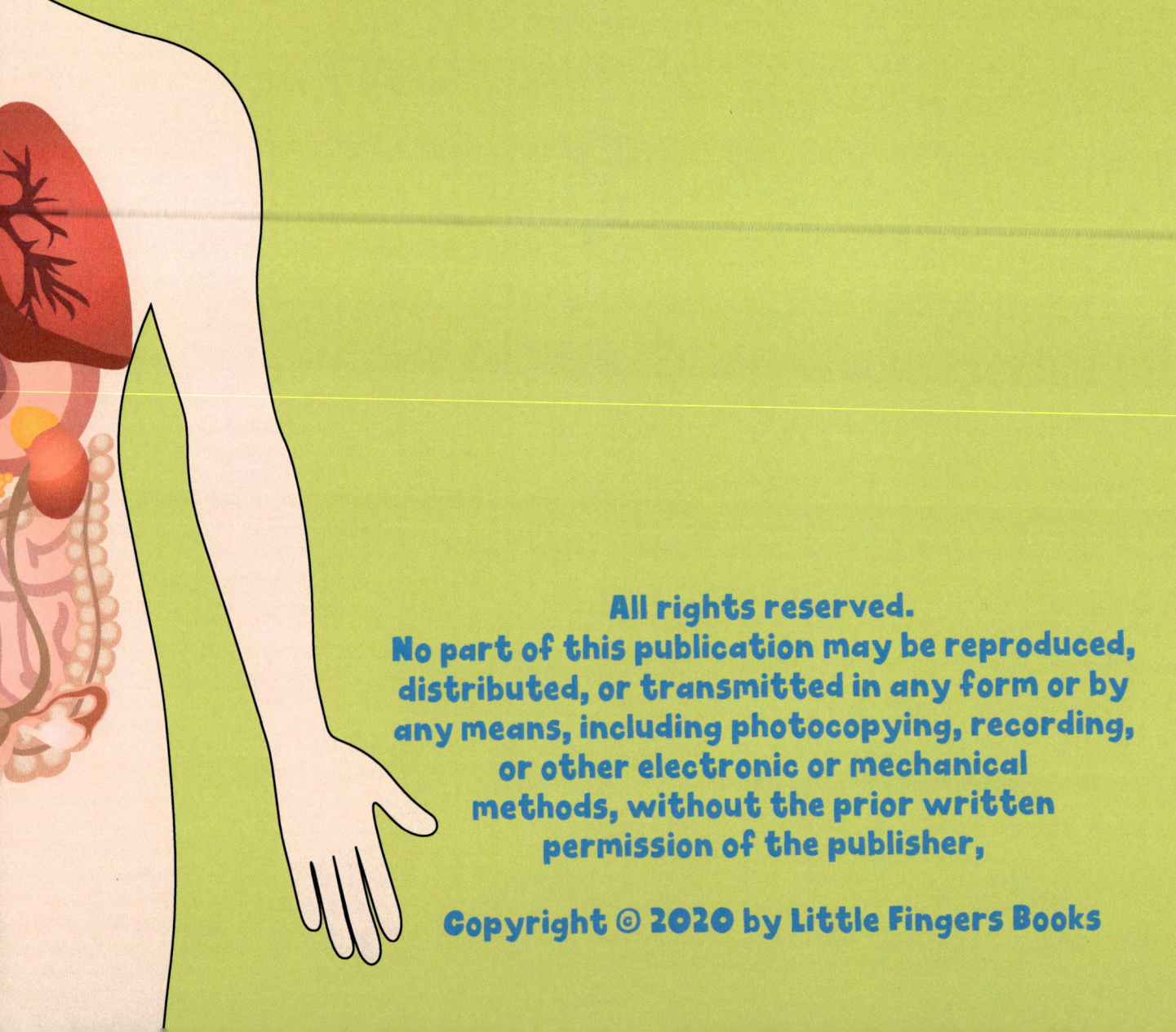

All rights reserved.
No part of this publication may be reproduced, distributed, or transmitted in any form or by any means, including photocopying, recording, or other electronic or mechanical methods, without the prior written permission of the publisher,

Copyright © 2020 by Little Fingers Books

Made in the USA
Monee, IL
13 November 2020